THE GREAT OPERAS OF
Wolfgang Amadeus Mozart

An Account of the Life and Work of this Distinguished Composer, with Particular Attention to his Operas.

Illustrated with Portraits in Costume and Scenes from Opera

By
GUSTAV KOBBÉ

Copyright © 2018 Read Books Ltd.
This book is copyright and may not be
reproduced or copied in any way without
the express permission of the publisher in writing

British Library Cataloguing-in-Publication Data
A catalogue record for this book is available from
the British Library

A History of The Theatre

'The Theatre' is a collaborative form of fine art that uses live performers to present the experience of a real or imagined event. The performers may communicate this experience to the audience through combinations of gesture, speech, song, music, and dance, with elements of art, stagecraft and set design used to enhance the physicality, presence and immediacy of the experience. The specific place of the performance is also named by the word 'theatre' – derived from the Ancient Greek word *théatron*, meaning 'a place for viewing', itself from *theáomai*, meaning 'to see', 'watch' or 'observe'.

Modern Western theatre largely derives from ancient Greek drama, from which it borrows technical terminology, classification into genres, and many of its themes, stock characters, and plot elements. The city-state of Athens is where 'theatre' as we know it originated, as part of a broader culture of theatricality and performance in classical Greece that included festivals, religious rituals, politics, law, athletics, music, poetry, weddings, funerals, and symposia. Participation in the city-state's many festivals – and attendance at the City Dionysia as an audience member (or even as a participant in the theatrical productions) in particular, was an important part of citizenship.

The theatre of ancient Greece consisted of three types of drama: tragedy, comedy, and the satyr play (a form of tragicomedy, similar in spirit to the bawdy satire of burlesque). The origins of theatre in ancient Greece, according to Aristotle (384–322 BCE), the first theoretician of theatre, are to be found in the festivals that honoured Dionysus. These performances (the aforementioned City Dionysia) were held in semi-circular auditoria cut into hillsides, capable of seating 10,000–20,000 people. The stage consisted of a dancing floor (orchestra), dressing room and scene-building area (skene). Since the words were the most important part, good acoustics and clear delivery were paramount. The actors (always men) wore masks appropriate to the characters they represented, and each might play several parts.

Athenian tragedy (the oldest surviving form of tragedy) emerged sometime during the sixth century BCE, and flowered during the fifth century BCE – from the end of which it began to spread throughout the Greek world – and continued in popularity until the beginning of the Hellenistic period. Aeschylus, Sophocles, and Euripides were masters of the genre. The other side of the coin – Athenian comedy, is conventionally divided into three periods; 'Old Comedy', 'Middle Comedy', and 'New Comedy'. Old Comedy survives today largely in the form of the eleven surviving plays of Aristophanes, while Middle Comedy is largely lost (preserved only in a few relatively short fragments in authors such as Athenaeus of Naucratis). New Comedy is known primarily from the substantial papyrus fragments of Menander.

Western theatre developed and expanded considerably under the Romans. The theatre of ancient Rome was a thriving and diverse art form, ranging from festival performances of street theatre, nude dancing, and acrobatics, to the staging of Plautus's broadly appealing situation comedies, to the high-style, verbally elaborate tragedies of Seneca. Although Rome had a native tradition of performance, the Hellenization of Roman culture in the third century BCE had a profound and energizing effect on Roman theatre and encouraged the development of Latin literature of the highest quality for the stage. This tradition fed into the modern theatre we know today, and during the renaissance, theatre generally moved away from the poetic drama of the Greeks, and towards a more naturalistic prose style of dialogue. By the nineteenth century and the Industrial Revolution, this trend continued to progress.

In England, theatre was immensely popular, but took a big pause during 1642 and 1660 because of Cromwell's Interregnum. Prior to this, 'English renaissance theatre' was witnessed, with celebrated playwrights such as William Shakespeare, Christopher Marlowe and Ben Jonson. Under Queen Elizabeth, drama was a unified expression as far as social class was concerned, and the Court watched the same plays the commoners saw in the public playhouses. With the development of the private theatres, drama became more oriented towards the tastes and values of an upper-class audience however. By the later part of the reign of Charles I, few new plays were being written for the public theatres, which sustained themselves on the accumulated works of the previous decades. Theatre was now seen as something sinful and the Puritans tried very hard to drive it out of their society. Due to this stagnant period, once Charles II came back to the throne in 1660, theatre (among other arts) exploded with influences from France, and the wider continent.

The eighteenth century saw the widespread introduction of women to the stage – a development previously unthinkable. These women were looked at as celebrities (also a newer concept, thanks to ideas on individualism that were beginning to be born in Renaissance Humanism) but on the other hand, it was still very new and revolutionary. Comedies were full of the young and very much in vogue, with the storyline following their love lives: commonly a young roguish hero professing his love to the chaste and free minded heroine near the end of the play, much like Sheridan's *The School for Scandal*. Many of the comedies were fashioned after the French tradition, mainly Molière (the great comedic playwright), again harking back to the French influence of the King and his court after their exile.

After this point, there was an explosion of theatrical styles. Throughout the nineteenth century, the popular theatrical forms of Romanticism, melodrama, Victorian burlesque and the well-made plays of Scribe and Sardou gave way to the problem plays of Naturalism and Realism; the farces of Feydeau; Wagner's operatic *Gesamtkunstwerk*; musical theatre (including Gilbert and Sullivan's operas); F. C. Burnand's, W. S. Gilbert's and Wilde's drawing-room comedies; Symbolism; proto-Expressionism in the late works of August Strindberg and Henrik Ibsen; and Edwardian musical comedy. The list continues! These trends continued through the twentieth century in the realism of Stanislavski and Lee Strasberg, the political theatre of Erwin Piscator and Bertolt Brecht, the so-called Theatre of the Absurd of Samuel Beckett and Eugène Ionesco, and the rise of American and British musicals.

Theatre itself has an incredibly long history, and despite the massive proliferation of theatrical styles and mediums – it essentially owes its existence to the ancient Greeks and the Romans. The three main genres; tragedy, comedy and satyre, continue to influence plot themes, directing, writing and acting, with frequent and fascinating interrelations and overlaps. As a genre, it remains as popular today as it has ever been, and continues as a massive influence on popular culture more broadly. It is hoped that the current reader enjoys this book on the subject.

Wolfgang Amadeus Mozart

(1756-1791)

THE operas of Gluck supplanted those of Lully and Rameau. Those of Mozart, while they did not supplant Gluck's, wrested from them the sceptre of supremacy. In a general way it may be said that, before Mozart's time, composers of grand opera reached back to antiquity and mythology, or to the early Christian era, for their subjects. Their works moved with a certain restricted grandeur. Their characters were remote.

Mozart's subjects were more modern, even contemporary. Moreover, he was one of the brightest stars in the musical firmament. His was a complete and easy mastery of all forms of music. "In his music breathes the warm-hearted, laughter-loving artist," writes Theodore Baker. That is a correct characterization. "The Marriage of Figaro" is still regarded as a model of what a comic grand opera, if so I may call it, should be. "Don Giovanni," despite its tragic *dénouement*, sparkles with humour, and *Don Giovanni* himself, despite the evil he does, is a jovial character. "The Magic Flute" is full of amusing incidents and, if its relationship to the rites of freemasonry has been correctly interpreted, was a contemporary subject of strong human interest, notwithstanding its story being laid in ancient Egypt. In fact it may be said that, in the evolution of opera, Mozart was the first to impart to it a strong human interest with humour playing about it like sunlight.

The Complete Opera Book

The libretto of "The Marriage of Figaro" was derived from a contemporary French comedy; "Don Giovanni," though its plot is taken from an old Spanish story, has in its principal character a type of libertine, whose reckless daring inspires loyalty not only in his servant, but even in at least one of his victims—a type as familiar to Mozart's contemporaries as it is to us; the probable contemporary significance of "The Magic Flute" I have already mentioned, and the point is further considered under the head of that opera.

For the most part as free from unnecessary vocal embellishments as are the operas of Gluck, Mozart, being the more gifted composer, attained an even higher degree of dramatic expression than his predecessor. May I say that he even gave to the voice a human clang it hitherto had lacked, and in this respect also advanced the art of opera? By this I mean that, full of dramatic significance as his voice parts are, they have, too, an ingratiating human quality which the music of his predecessor lacks. In plasticity of orchestration his operas also mark a great advance.

Excepting a few works by Gluck, every opera before Mozart and the operas of every composer contemporary with him, and for a considerable period after him, have disappeared from the repertoire. The next two operas to hold the stage, Beethoven's "Fidelio" (in its final form) and Rossini's "Barber of Seville" were not produced until 1814 and 1816—respectively twenty-three and twenty-five years after Mozart's death.

That Mozart was a genius by the grace of God will appear from the simple statement that his career came to an end at the age of thirty-five. Compare this with the long careers of the three other composers, whose influence upon opera was supreme—Gluck, Wagner, and Verdi. Gluck died in his seventy-third year, Wagner in his seven-

Wolfgang Amadeus Mozart

tieth, and Verdi in his eighty-eighth. Yet the composer who laid down his pen and went to a pauper's grave at thirty-five, contributed as much as any of these to the evolution of the art of opera.

LE NOZZE DI FIGARO

THE MARRIAGE OF FIGARO

Opera in four acts by Mozart; words by Lorenzo da Ponte, after Beaumarchais. Produced at the National Theatre, Vienna, May 1, 1786, Mozart conducting. Académie de Musique, Paris, as "Le Mariage de Figaro" (with Beaumarchais's dialogue), 1793; as "Les Noces de Figaro" (words by Barbier and Carré), 1858. London, in Italian, King's Theatre, June 18, 1812. New York, 1823, with T. Phillips, of Dublin, as *Figaro;* May 10, 1824, with Pearman as *Figaro* and Mrs. Holman, as *Susanna;* January 18, 1828, with Elizabeth Alston, as *Susanna;* all these were in English and at the Park Theatre. (See concluding paragraph of this article.) Notable revivals in Italian, at the Metropolitan Opera House: 1902, with Sembrich, Eames, Fritzi Scheff, de Reszke, and Campanari; 1909, Sembrich, Eames, Farrar, and Scotti; 1916, Hempel, Matzenauer, Farrar, and Scotti.

CHARACTERS

COUNT ALMAVIVA	*Baritone*
FIGARO, his valet	*Baritone*
DOCTOR BARTOLO, a Physician	*Bass*
DON BASILIO, a music-master	*Tenor*
CHERUBINO, a page	*Soprano*
ANTONIO, a gardener	*Bass*
DON CURZIO, counsellor at law	*Tenor*
COUNTESS ALMAVIVA	*Soprano*
SUSANNA, her personal maid, affianced to FIGARO	*Soprano*
MARCELLINA, a duenna	*Soprano*
BARBARINA, ANTONIO'S daughter	*Soprano*

Time—17th Century   *Place*—The Count's chateau of Aguas Frescas, near Seville.

"Le Nozze di Figaro" was composed by Mozart by command of Emperor Joseph II., of Austria. After congratulating the composer at the end of the first performance, the Emperor said to him: "You must admit, however, my dear Mozart, that there are a great many notes in your score." "Not one too many, Sire," was Mozart's reply.

(The anecdote, it should be noted, also, is told of the first performance of Mozart's "Cosi Fan Tutti.")

No opera composed before "Le Nozze di Figaro" can be compared with it for development of ensemble, charm and novelty of melody, richness and variety of orchestration. Yet Mozart composed this score in a month. The finale to the second act occupied him but two days. In the music the sparkle of high comedy alternates with the deeper sentiment of the affections.

Michael Kelly, the English tenor, who was the *Basilio* and *Curzio* in the original production, tells in his memoirs of the splendid sonority with which Benucci, the *Figaro*, sang the martial "Non più andrai" at the first orchestral rehearsal. Mozart, who was on the stage in a crimson pelisse and cocked hat trimmed with gold lace, kept repeating *sotto voce*, "Bravo, bravo, Benucci!" At the conclusion the orchestra and all on the stage burst into applause and vociferous acclaim of Mozart:

"Bravo, bravo, Maestro! Viva, viva, grande Mozart!"

Further, the *Reminiscences* of Kelly inform us of the enthusiastic reception of "Le Nozze di Figaro" upon its production, almost everything being encored, so that the time required for its performance was nearly doubled. Notwithstanding this success, it was withdrawn after comparatively few representations, owing to Italian intrigue at the court and opera, led by Mozart's rival, the composer Salieri—now heard of only because of that rivalry. In Prague, where the opera was produced in January, 1787, its success was so great that Bondini, the manager of the company, was able to persuade Mozart to compose

Wolfgang Amadeus Mozart

an opera for first performance in Prague. The result was "Don Giovanni."

The story of "Le Nozze di Figaro" is a sequel to that of "The Barber of Seville," which Rossini set to music. Both are derived from "Figaro" comedies by Beaumarchais. In Rossini's opera it is *Figaro*, at the time a barber in Seville, who plays the go-between for *Count Almaviva* and his beloved *Rosina, Dr. Bartolo's* pretty ward. *Rosina* is now the wife of the *Count*, who unfortunately, is promiscuous in his attentions to women, including *Susanna*, the *Countess's* vivacious maid, who is affianced to *Figaro*. The latter and the music-master *Basilio* who, in their time helped to hoodwink *Bartolo*, are in the service of the *Count*, *Figaro* having been rewarded with the position of valet and major-domo. *Bartolo*, for whom, as formerly, *Marcellina* is keeping house, still is *Figaro's* enemy, because of the latter's interference with his plans to marry *Rosina* and so secure her fortune to himself. The other characters in the opera also belong to the personnel of the *Count's* household.

Aside from the difference between Rossini's and Mozart's scores, which are alike only in that each opera is a masterpiece of the comic sentiment, there is at least one difference between the stories. In Rossini's "Barber" *Figaro*, a man, is the mainspring of the action. In Mozart's opera it is *Susanna*, a woman; and a clever woman may possess in the rôle of protagonist in comedy a chicness and sparkle quite impossible to a man. The whole plot of "Le Nozze di Figaro" plays around *Susanna's* efforts to nip in the bud the intrigue in which the *Count* wishes to engage her. She is aided by the *Countess* and by *Figaro;* but she still must appear to encourage while evading the *Count's* advances, and do so without offending him, lest both she and her affianced be made to suffer through his disfavour. In the libretto there is much that is *risqué*,

The Complete Opera Book

suggestive. But as the average opera goer does not understand the subtleties of the Italian language, and the average English translation is too clumsy to preserve them, it is quite possible—especially in this advanced age—to attend a performance of "Le Nozze di Figaro" without imperilling one's morals.

There is a romping overture. Then, in Act I, we learn that *Figaro, Count Almaviva's* valet, wants to get married. *Susanna*, the *Countess's* maid, is the chosen one. The *Count* has assigned to them a room near his, ostensibly because his valet will be able to respond quickly to his summons. The room is the scene of this Act. *Susanna* tells her lover that the true reason for the *Count's* choice of their room is the fact that their noble master is running after her. Now *Figaro* is willing enough to "play up" for the little *Count*, if he should take it into his head "to venture on a little dance" once too often. ("Si vuol ballare, Signor Contino!")

Unfortunately, however, *Figaro* himself is in a fix. He has borrowed money from *Marcellina*, *Bartolo's* housekeeper, and he has promised to marry her in case of his inability to repay her. She now appears, to demand of *Figaro* the fulfilment of his promise. *Bartolo* encourages her in this, both out of spite against *Figaro* and because he wants to be rid of the old woman, who has been his mistress and even borne him a son, who, however, was kidnapped soon after his birth. There is a vengeance aria for *Bartolo*, and a spiteful duet for *Marcellina* and *Susanna*, beginning: "Via resti servita, madama brillante" (Go first, I entreat you, Miss, model of beauty!).

The next scene opens between the page, *Cherubino*, a

Wolfgang Amadeus Mozart

boy in love with every petticoat, and *Susanna*. He begs *Susanna* to intercede for him with the *Count*, who has dismissed him. *Cherubino* desires to stay around the *Countess*, for whom he has conceived one of his grand passions. "Non so più cosa son, cosa faccio"—(Ah, what feelings now possess me!) The *Count's* step is heard. *Cherubino* hides himself behind a chair, from where he hears the *Count* paying court to *Susanna*. The voice of the music-master then is heard from without. The *Count* moves toward the door. *Cherubino*, taking advantage of this, slips out from behind the chair and conceals himself in it under a dress that has been thrown over it. The *Count*, however, instead of going out, hides behind the chair, in the same place where *Cherubino* has been. *Basilio*, who has entered, now makes all kinds of malicious remarks and insinuations about the flirtations of *Cherubino* with *Susanna* and also with the *Countess*. The *Count*, enraged at the free use of his wife's name, emerges from behind the chair. Only the day before, he says, he has caught that rascal, *Cherubino*, with the gardener's daughter *Barbarina* (with whom the *Count* also is flirting). *Cherubino*, he continues, was hidden under a coverlet, "just as if under this dress here." Then, suiting the action to the words, by way of demonstration, he lifts the gown from the chair, and lo! there is *Cherubino*. The *Count* is furious. But as the page has overheard him making love to *Susanna*, and as *Figaro* and others have come in to beg that he be forgiven, the *Count*, while no longer permitting him to remain in the castle, grants him an officer's commission in his own regiment. It is here that *Figaro* addresses *Cherubino* in the dashing martial air, "Non più andrai, farfallone amoroso" (Play no more, the part of a lover).

Act II. Still, the *Count*, for whom the claims of *Marcellina* upon *Figaro* have come in very opportunely, has not given consent for his valet's wedding. He wishes to

The Complete Opera Book

carry his own intrigue with *Susanna*, the genuineness of whose love for *Figaro* he underestimates, to a successful issue. *Susanna* and *Figaro* meet in the *Countess's* room. The *Countess* has been soliloquizing upon love, of whose fickleness the *Count* has but provided too many examples. —"Porgi amor, qual che ristoro" (Love, thou holy ,purest passion.) *Figaro* has contrived a plan to gain the consent of the *Count* to his wedding with *Susanna*. The valet's scheme is to make the *Count* ashamed of his own flirtations. *Figaro* has sent a letter to the *Count*, which divulges a supposed rendezvous of the *Countess* in the garden. At the same time *Susanna* is to make an appointment to meet the *Count* in the same spot. But, in place of *Susanna*, *Cherubino*, dressed in *Susanna's* clothes, will meet the *Count*. Both will be caught by the *Countess* and the *Count* thus be confounded.

Cherubino is then brought in to try on *Susanna's* clothes. He sings to the *Countess* an air of sentiment, one of the famous vocal numbers of the opera, the exquisite: "Voi che sapete, che cosa è amor" (What is this feeling makes me so sad).

The *Countess*, examining his officer's commission, finds that the seal to it has been forgotten. While in the midst of these proceedings someone knocks. It is the *Count*. Consternation. *Cherubino* flees into the *Countess's* room and *Susanna* hides behind a curtain. The evident embarrassment of his wife arouses the suspicions of her husband, who, gay himself, is very jealous of her. He tries the door *Cherubino* has bolted from the inside, then goes off to get tools to break it down with. He takes his wife with him. While he is away, *Cherubino* slips out and leaps out of a window into the garden. In his place,

Wolfgang Amadeus Mozart

Susanna bolts herself in the room, so that, when the *Count* breaks open the door, it is only to discover that *Susanna* is in his wife's room. All would be well, but unfortunately *Antonio*, the gardener, enters. A man, he says, has jumped out of the *Countess's* window and broken a flowerpot. *Figaro*, who has come in, and who senses that something has gone wrong, says that it was he who was with *Susanna* and jumped out of the window. But the gardener has found a paper. He shows it. It is *Cherubino's* commission. How did *Figaro* come by it? The *Countess* whispers something to *Figaro*. Ah, yes; *Cherubino* handed it to him in order that he should obtain the missing seal.

Everything appears to be cleared up when *Marcellina*, accompanied by *Bartolo*, comes to lodge formal complaint against *Figaro* for breach of promise, which for the *Count* is a much desired pretext to refuse again his consent to *Figaro's* wedding with *Susanna*. These, the culminating episodes of this act, form a finale which is justly admired, a finale so gradually developed and so skilfully evolved that, although only the principals participate in it, it is as effective as if it employed a full ensemble of soloists, chorus, and orchestra worked up in the most elaborate fashion. Indeed, for effectiveness produced by simple means, the operas of Mozart are models.

But to return to the story. At the trial in Act III, between *Marcellina* and *Figaro*, it develops that *Figaro* is her long-lost natural son. *Susanna* pays the costs of the trial and nothing now seems to stand in the way of her union with *Figaro*. The *Count*, however, is not yet entirely cured of his fickle fancies. So the *Countess* and *Susanna* hit upon still another scheme in this play of complications. During the wedding festivities *Susanna* is to contrive to send secretly to the *Count* a note, in which she invites him to meet her. Then the *Countess* dressed in *Susanna's* clothes, is to meet him at the place named. *Figaro* knows

The Complete Opera Book

nothing of this plan. Chancing to find out about the note, he too becomes jealous—another, though minor, contribution to the mixup of emotions. In this act the concoction of the letter by the *Countess* and *Susanna* is the basis of the most beautiful vocal number in the opera, the "letter duet" or Canzonetta sull' aria (the "Canzonetta of the Zephyr")—"Che soave zeffiretto" (Hither gentle zephyr); an exquisite melody, in which the lady dictates, the maid writes down, and the voices of both blend in comment.

The final Act brings about the desired result after a series of amusing *contretempts* in the garden. The *Count* sinks on his knees before his *Countess* and, as the curtain falls, there is reason to hope that he is prepared to mend his ways.

Regarding the early performances of "Figaro" in this country, these early performances were given "with Mozart's music, but adapted by Henry Rowley Bishop." When I was a boy, a humorous way of commenting upon an artistic sacrilege was to exclaim: "Ah! Mozart improved by Bishop!" I presume the phrase came down from these early representations of "The Marriage of Figaro." Bishop was the composer of "Home, Sweet Home." In 1839 his wife eloped with Bochsa, the harp virtuoso, afterwards settled in New York, and for many years sang in concert and taught under the name of Mme. Anna Bishop.

DON GIOVANNI

Opera in two acts by Mozart; text by Lorenzo da Ponte. Productions, Prague, Oct. 29, 1787; Vienna, May 17, 1788; London, April 12, 1817; New York, Park Theatre, May 23, 1826.
Original title: "Il Dissoluto Punito, ossia il Don Giovanni" (The

SCOTTI AS DON GIOVANNI.

SEMBRICH AS ZERLINA IN "DON GIOVANNI."

Wolfgang Amadeus Mozart

Reprobate Punished, or Don Giovanni). The work was originally characterized as an *opera buffa*, or *dramma giocoso*, but Mozart's noble setting lifted it out of that category.

Characters

Don Pedro, the Commandant	*Bass*
Donna Anna, his daughter	*Soprano*
Don Ottavio, her betrothed	*Tenor*
Don Giovanni	*Baritone*
Leporello, his servant	*Bass*
Donna Elvira	*Soprano*
Zerlina	*Soprano*
Masetto, betrothed to Zerlina	*Tenor*

"Don Giovanni" was presented for the first time in Prague, because Mozart, satisfied with the manner in which Bondini's troupe had sung his "Marriage of Figaro" a little more than a year before, had agreed to write another work for the same house.

The story on which da Ponte based his libretto—the statue of a murdered man accepting an insolent invitation to banquet with his murderer, appearing at the feast and dragging him down to hell—is very old. It goes back to the Middle Ages, probably further. A French authority considers that da Ponte derived his libretto from " Le Festin de Pierre," Molière's version of the old tale. Da Ponte, however, made free use of "Il Convitato di Pietra" (The Stone-Guest), a libretto written by the Italian theatrical poet Bertati for the composer Giuseppe Gazzaniga. Whoever desires to follow up this interesting phase of the subject will find the entire libretto of Bertati's "Convitato" reprinted, with a learned commentary by Chrysander, in volume iv of the *Vierteljahrheft für Musikwissenschaft* (Music Science Quarterly), a copy of which is in the New York Public Library.

Mozart agreed to hand over the finished score in time for the autumn season of 1787, for the sum of one hundred

The Complete Opera Book

ducats ($240). Richard Strauss receives for a new opera a guarantee of ten performances at a thousand dollars—$10,000 in all—and, of course, his royalties thereafter. There is quite a distinction in these matters between the eighteenth century and the present. And what a lot of good a few thousand dollars would have done the impecunious composer of the immortal "Don Giovanni!" Also, one is tempted to ask oneself if any modern ten thousand dollar opera will live as long as the two hundred and forty dollar one which already is 130 years old.

Bondini's company, for which Mozart wrote his masterpiece of dramatic music, furnished the following cast: *Don Giovanni*, Signor Bassi, twenty-two years old, a fine baritone, an excellent singer and actor; *Donna Anna*, Signora Teresa Saporiti; *Donna Elvira*, Signora Catarina Micelli, who had great talent for dramatic expression; *Zerlina*, Signora Teresa Bondini, wife of the manager; *Don Ottavio*, Signor Antonio Baglioni, with a sweet, flexible tenor voice; *Leporello*, Signor Felice Ponziani, an excellent basso comico; *Don Pedro* (the Commandant), and *Masetto*, Signor Giuseppe Lolli.

Mozart directed the rehearsals, had the singers come to his house to study, gave them advice how some of the difficult passages should be executed, explained the characters they represented, and exacted finish, detail, and accuracy. Sometimes he even chided the artists for an Italian impetuosity, which might be out of keeping with the charm of his melodies. At the first rehearsal, however, not being satisfied with the way in which Signora Bondini gave *Zerlina's* cry of terror from behind the scenes, when the *Don* is supposed to attempt her ruin, Mozart left the orchestra and went upon the stage. Ordering the first act finale to be repeated from the minuet on, he concealed himself in the wings. There, in the peasant dress of *Zerlina*, with its short skirt, stood Signora Bondini, waiting

Wolfgang Amadeus Mozart

for her cue. When it came, Mozart quickly reached out a hand from his place of concealment and pinched her leg. She gave a piercing shriek. "There! That is how I want it," he said, emerging from the wings, while the Bondini, not knowing whether to laugh or blush, did both.

One of the most striking features of the score, the warning words which the statue of the *Commandant*, in the plaza before the cathedral of Seville, utters within the hearing of *Don Giovanni* and *Leporello*, was originally accompanied by the trombones only. At rehearsal in Prague, Mozart not satisfied with the way the passage was played, stepped over toward the desks at which the trombonists sat.

One of them spoke up: "It can't be played any better. Even you couldn't teach us how."

Mozart smiled. "Heaven forbid," he said, "that I should attempt to teach you how to play the trombone. But let me have the parts."

Looking them over he immediately made up his mind what to do. With a few quick strokes of the pen, he added the wood-wind instruments as they are now found in the score.

It is well known that the overture of "Don Giovanni" was written almost on the eve of the first performance. Mozart passed a gay evening with some friends. One of them said to him: "Tomorrow the first performance of 'Don Giovanni' will take place, and you have not yet composed the overture!" Mozart pretended to get nervous about it and withdrew to his room, where he found music-paper, pens, and ink. He began to compose about midnight. Whenever he grew sleepy, his wife, who was by his side, entertained him with stories to keep him awake. It is said that it took him but three hours to produce this overture.

The next evening, a little before the curtain rose, the copyists finished transcribing the parts for the orchestra.

The Complete Opera Book

Hardly had they brought the sheets, still wet, to the theatre, when Mozart, greeted by enthusiastic applause, entered the orchestra and took his seat at the piano. Although the musicians had not had time to rehearse the overture, they played it with such precision that the audience broke out into fresh applause. As the curtain rose and *Leporello* came forward to sing his solo, Mozart laughingly whispered to the musicians near him: "Some notes fell under the stands. But it went well."

The overture consists of an introduction which reproduces the scene of the banquet at which the statue appears. It is followed by an allegro which characterizes the impetuous, pleasure-seeking *Don*, oblivious to consequences. It reproduces the dominant character of the opera.

Without pause, Mozart links up the overture with the song of *Leporello*. The four principal personages of the opera appear early in the proceedings. The tragedy which brings them together so soon and starts the action, gives an effective touch of fore-ordained retribution to the misdeeds upon which *Don Giovanni* so gaily enters. This early part of the opera divides itself into four episodes. Wrapped in his cloak and seated in the garden of a house in Seville, Spain, which *Don Giovanni*, on amorous adventure bent, has entered secretly during the night—it is the residence of the *Commandant*—*Leporello* is complaining of the fate which makes him a servant to such a restless and dangerous master. "Notte e giorno faticar" (Never rest by day or night), runs his song.

Don Giovanni hurriedly issues from the house, pursued by *Donna Anna*. There follows a trio in which the wrath of the insulted woman, the annoyance of the libertine, and the cowardice of *Leporello* are expressed simultaneously and in turn in manner most admirable. The *Commandant* attracted by the disturbance, arrives, draws his sword, and a duel ensues. In the unequal combat between the

Wolfgang Amadeus Mozart

aged *Commandant* and the agile *Don*, the *Commandant* receives a fatal wound. The trio which follows between *Don Giovanni*, the dying *Commandant*, and *Leporello* is a unique passage in the history of musical art. The genius of Mozart, tender, profound, pathetic, religious, is revealed in its entirety. Written in a solemn rhythm and in the key of F minor, so appropriate to dispose the mind to a gentle sadness, this trio, which fills only eighteen measures, contains in a restricted outline, but in master-strokes, the fundamental idea of this mysterious drama of crime and retribution. While the *Commandant* is breathing his last, emitting notes broken by long pauses, *Donna Anna*, who, during the duel between her father and *Don Giovanni*, has hurried off for help, returns accompanied by her servants and by *Don Ottavio*, her affianced. She utters a cry of terror at seeing the dead body of her father. The recitative which expresses her despair is intensely dramatic. The duet which she sings with *Don Ottavio* is both impassioned and solicitous, impetuous on her part, solicitous on his; for the rôle of *Don Ottavio* is stamped with the delicacy of sentiment, the respectful reserve of a well-born youth who is consoling the woman who is to be his wife. The passage, "Lascia, O cara, la rimembrenza amore!" (Through love's devotion, dear one) is of peculiar beauty in musical expression.

After *Donna Anna* and *Don Ottavio* have left, there enters *Donna Elvira*. The air she sings expresses a complicated nuance of passion. *Donna Elvira* is another of *Don Giovanni's* deserted ones. There are in the tears of this woman not only the grief of one who has been loved and now implores heaven for comfort, but also the indignation of one who has been deserted and betrayed. When she cries with emotion: "Ah! qui mi dice mai quel barbaro dov'è?" (In memory still lingers his love's delusive sway) one feels that, in spite of her outbursts of anger, she is ready to for-

The Complete Opera Book

give, if only a regretful smile shall recall to her the man who was able to charm her.

Don Giovanni hears from afar the voice of a woman in tears. He approaches, saying: "Cerchiam di consolare il suo tormento" (I must seek to console her sorrow). "Ah! yes," murmurs *Leporello*, under his breath: "Cosi ne consolò mille e otto cento" (He has consoled fully eighteen hundred). *Leporello* is charged by *Don Giovanni*, who, recognizing *Donna Elvira*, hurries away, to explain to her the reasons why he deserted her. The servant fulfils his mission as a complaisant valet. For it is here that he sings the "Madamina" air, which is so famous, and in which he relates with the skill of a historian the numerous amours of his master in the different parts of the world.

The "Air of Madamina," "Madamina! il catalogo" —(Dear lady, the catalogue) is a perfect passage of its kind; an exquisite mixture of grace and finish, of irony and sentiment, of comic declamation and melody, the whole enhanced by the poetry and skill of the accessories. There is nothing too much, nothing too little; no excess of detail to mar the whole. Every word is illustrated by the composer's imagination without his many brilliant sallies injuring the general effect. According to *Leporello's* catalogue his master's adventures in love have numbered 2065. To these Italy has contributed 245, Germany 231, France 100, Turkey 91, and Spain, his native land, 1003. The recital enrages *Donna Elvira*. She vows vengeance upon her betrayer.

The scene changes to the countryside of *Don Giovanni's* palace near Seville. A troop of gay peasants is seen arriving. The young and pretty *Zerlina* with *Masetto*, her affianced, and their friends are singing and dancing in honour of their approaching marriage. *Don Giovanni* and *Leporello* join this gathering of light-hearted and simple

Wolfgang Amadeus Mozart

young people. Having cast covetous eyes upon *Zerlina*, and having aroused her vanity and her spirit of coquetry by polished words of gallantry, the *Don* orders *Leporello* to get rid of the jealous *Masetto* by taking the entire gathering—excepting, of course, *Zerlina*—to his *château*. *Leporello* grumbles, but carries out his master's order. The latter, left alone with *Zerlina*, sings a duet with her which is one of the gems, not alone of this opera, but of opera in general: "Là ci darem la mano!" (Your hand in mine, my dearest). *Donna Elvira* appears and by her denunciation of *Don Giovanni*, "Ah! fuggi il traditore," makes clear to *Zerlina* the character of her fascinating admirer. *Donna Anna* and *Don Ottavio* come upon the stage and sing a quartette which begins: "Non ti fidar, o misera, di quel ribaldo cor" (Place not thy trust, O mourning one, in this polluted soul), at the end of which *Donna Anna*, as *Don Giovanni* departs, recognizes in his accents the voice of her father's assassin. Her narrative of the events of that terrible night is a declamatory recitative "in style as bold and as tragic as the finest recitatives of Gluck."

Don Giovanni orders preparations for the festival in his palace. He gives his commands to *Leporello* in the "Champagne aria," "Fin, ch' han dal vino" (Wine, flow a fountain), which is almost breathless with exuberance of anticipated revel. Then there is the ingratiating air of *Zerlina* begging *Masetto's* forgiveness for having flirted with the *Don*, "Batti, batti, o bel Masetto" (Chide me, chide me, dear Masetto), a number of enchanting grace, followed

by a brilliantly triumphant allegro, "Pace, pace o vita mia" (Love, I see you're now relenting).

The finale to the first act of "Don Giovanni" rightly passes for one of the masterpieces of dramatic music. *Lepo-*

The Complete Opera Book

rello, having opened a window to let the fresh evening air enter the palace hall, the violins of a small orchestra within are heard in the first measures of the graceful minuet. *Leporello* sees three maskers, two women and a man, outside. In accordance with custom they a e bidden to enter. *Don Giovanni* does not know that they are *Donna Anna, Donna Elvira,* and *Don Ottavio,* bent upon seeking the murderer of the *Commandant* and bringing him to justice. But even had he been aware of their purpose it probably would have made no difference, for courage this dissolute character certainly had.

After a moment of hesitation, after having taken council together, and repressing a movement of horror which they feel at the sight of the man whose crimes have darkened their lives, *Donna Elvira, Donna Anna,* and *Don Ottavio* decide to carry out their undertaking at all cost and to whatever end. Before entering the *château,* they pause on the threshold and, their souls moved by a holy fear, they address Heaven in one of the most touching prayers written by the hand of man. It is the number known throughout the world of music as the "Trio of the Masks," "Protegga, il giusto cielo"—(Just Heaven, now defend us)—one of those rare passages which, by its clearness of form, its elegance of musical diction, and its profundity of sentiment, moves the layman and charms the connoisseur.

The festivities begin with the familiar minuet. Its graceful rhythm is prolonged indefinitely as a fundamental

Wolfgang Amadeus Mozart

idea, while in succession, two small orchestras on the stage, take up, one a rustic quadrille in double time, the other a waltz. Notwithstanding the differences in rhythm, the three dances are combined with a skill that piques the ear and excites admiration. The scene would be even more natural and entertaining than it usually is, if the orchestras on the stage always followed the direction *accordano* (tune up) which occurs in the score eight bars before each begins to play its dance, and if the dances themselves were carried out according to directions. Only the ladies and gentlemen should engage in the minuet, the peasants in the quadrille; and before *Don Giovanni* leads off *Zerlina* into an adjoining room he should have taken part with her in this dance, while *Leporello* seeks to divert the jealous *Masetto's* attention by seizing him in an apparent exuberance of spirits and insisting on dancing the waltz with him. *Masetto's* suspicions, however, are not to be allayed. He breaks away from *Leporello*. The latter hurries to warn his master. But just as he has passed through the door, *Zerlina's* piercing shriek for help is heard from within. *Don Giovanni* rushes out, sword in hand, dragging out with him none other than poor *Leporello*, whom he has opportunely seized in the entrance, and whom, under pretence that he is the guilty party, he threatens to kill in order to turn upon him the suspicion that rests upon himself. But this ruse fails to deceive any one. *Donna Anna, Donna Elvira,* and *Don Ottavio* unmask and accuse *Don Giovanni* of the murder of the *Commandant;* "Tutto già si sà" (Everything is known and you are recognized). Taken aback, at first, *Don Giovanni* soon recovers himself. Turning, at bay, he defies the enraged crowd. A storm is rising without. A storm sweeps over the orchestra. Thunder growls in the basses, lightning plays on the fiddles. *Don Giovanni*, cool, intrepid, cuts a passage through the crowd upon which, at the same time,

The Complete Opera Book

he hurls his contempt. (In a performance at the Academy of Music, New York, about 1872, I saw *Don Giovanni* stand off the crowd with a pistol.)

The second act opens with a brief duet between *Don Giovanni* and *Leporello*. The trio which follows: "Ah! taci, ingiusto core" (Ah, silence, heart rebellious), for *Donna Elvira, Leporello*, and *Don Giovanni*, is an exquisite passage. *Donna Elvira*, leaning sadly on a balcony, allows her melancholy regrets to wander in the pale moonlight which envelops her figure in a semi-transparent gloom. In spite of the scene which she has recently witnessed, in spite of wrongs she herself has endured, she cannot hate *Don Giovanni* or efface his image from her heart. Her reward is that her recreant lover in the darkness below, changes costume with his servant and while *Leporello*, disguised as the *Don*, attracts *Donna Elvira* into the garden, the cavalier himself addresses to *Zerlina*, who has been taken under *Donna Elvira's* protection, the charming serenade: "Deh! vieni alla finestra" (Appear, love at thy window), which he accompanies on the mandolin, or should so accompany, for usually the accompaniment is played pizzicato by the orchestra.

As the result of complications, which I shall not attempt to follow, *Masetto*, who is seeking to administer physical chastisement to *Don Giovanni*, receives instead a drubbing from the latter.

Zerlina, while by no means indifferent to the attentions of the dashing *Don*, is at heart faithful to *Masetto* and, while I fancy she is by no means obtuse to the humorous aspect of his chastisement by *Don Giovanni*, she comes trippingly out of the house and consoles the poor fellow with the graceful measures of "Vedrai carino, se sei buonino" (List, and I'll find love, if you are kind love).

Shortly after this episode comes *Don Ottavio's* famous air, the solo number which makes the rôle worth while,

Wolfgang Amadeus Mozart

"Il mio tesoro intanti" (Fly then, my love, entreating). Upon this air praise has been exhausted. It has been called the "pietra di paragone" of tenors—the touchstone, the supreme test of classic song.

Retribution upon *Don Giovanni* is not to be too long deferred. After the escapade of the serenade and the drubbing of *Masetto*, the *Don*, who has made off, chances to meet in the churchyard (or in the public square) with *Leporello*, who meanwhile has gotten rid of *Donna Elvira*. It is about two in the morning. They see the newly erected statue to the murdered *Commandant*. *Don Giovanni* bids it, through *Leporello*, to supper with him in his palace. Will it accept? The statue answers, "Yea!" *Leporello* is terrified. And *Don Giovanni*?

"In truth the scene is bizarre. The old boy comes to supper. Now hasten and bestir yourself to spread a royal feast."

Such is the sole reflection that the fateful miracle, to which he has just been a witness, draws from this miscreant, who, whatever else he may be, is brave.

Back in his palace, *Don Giovanni* seats himself at table and sings of the pleasures of life. An orchestra on the stage plays airs from Vincente Martino's "Una Cosa Rara" (A Rare Thing); Sarti's "Fra Due Litiganti" (Between Two Litigants), and Mozart's own "Nozze di Figaro," *Leporello* announcing the selections. The "Figaro" air is "Non più andrai" (Play no more, boy, the part of a lover).

Donna Elvira enters. On her knees she begs the man who has betrayed her to mend his ways. Her plea falls on deaf ears. She leaves. Her shriek is heard from the corridor. She re-enters and flees the palace by another door.

The Complete Opera Book

"Va, veder che cos' è stato" (Go, and see what it is) *Don Giovanni* commands *Leporello*.

The latter returns trembling with fright. He has seen in the corridor "l'uom di sasso, l'uomo bianco"—the man of stone, the big white man.

Seizing a candle, drawing his sword, *Don Giovanni* boldly goes into the corridor. A few moments later he backs into the room, receding before the statue of the *Commandant*. The lights go out. All is dark save for the flame of the candle in *Don Giovanni's* hand. Slowly, with heavy footsteps that re-echo, the statue enters. It speaks.

"Don Giovanni, you have invited me to sit at table with you. Lo! I am here."

Well knowing the fate in store for him, yet, with unebbing courage, *Don Giovanni* nonchalantly commands *Leporello* to serve supper.

"Desist!" exclaims the statue. "He who has sat at a heavenly banquet, does not break the bread of mortals. . . . Don Giovanni, will you come to sup with me?"

"I will," fearlessly answers the *Don*.

"Give me your hand in gage thereof."

"Here it is."

Don Giovanni extends his hand. The statue's huge hand of stone closes upon it.

"Huh! what an icy grasp!"—"Repent! Change your course at your last hour."—"No, far from me such a thought."—"Repent, O miscreant!"—"No, you old fool." —"Repent!"—"No!"

Nothing daunts him. A fiery pit opens. Demons seize him—unrepentant to the end—and drag him down.

The music of the scene is gripping, yet accomplished without an addition to the ordinary orchestra of Mozart's day, without straining after effect, without any means save those commonly to his hand.

In the modern opera house the final curtain falls upon

Scotti as Don Giovanni.

Wolfgang Amadeus Mozart

this scene. In the work, however, there is another scene in which the other characters moralize upon *Don Giovanni's* end. There is one accusation, however, none can urge against him. He was not a coward. Therein lies the appeal of the character. His is a brilliant, impetuous figure, with a dash of philosophy, which is that, sometime, somewhere, in the course of his amours, he will discover the perfect woman from whose lips he will be able to draw the sweetness of all women. Moreover he is a villain with a keen sense of humour. Inexcusable in real life, he is a debonair, fascinating figure on the stage, whereas *Donna Anna*, *Donna Elvira*, and *Don Ottavio* are mere hinges in the drama and as creations purely musical. *Zerlina*, on the other hand, is one of Mozart's most delectable characters. *Leporello*, too, is clearly drawn, dramatically and musically; a coward, yet loyal to the master who appeals to a strain of the humorous in him and whose courage he admires.

For the Vienna production Mozart wrote three new vocal numbers, which are printed in the score as additions. Caterina Cavalieri, the *Elvira*, had complained to Mozart, that the Viennese public did not appreciate her as did audiences of other cities and begged him for something that would give her voice full scope. The result was the fine aria: "Mi tradi quell' alma ingrata." The *Ottavio*, Signor Morello, was considered unequal to "Il mio tesoro," so Mozart wrote the less exacting "Della sua pace," for him. To amuse the public he inserted a comic duet, "Per queste tue manine," for *Zerlina* and *Leporello*. This usually is omitted. The other two inserts were interpolated in the second act of the opera before the finale. In the Metropolitan Opera House version, however, *Donna Elvira* sings "Mi tradi" to express her rage after the "Madamina" of Leporello; and *Don Ottavio* sings "Della sua pace" before the scene in *Don Giovanni's* château.

The first performance of "Don Giovanni" in America

The Complete Opera Book

took place in the Park Theatre, New York, on Tuesday evening, May 23, 1826. I have verified the date in the file of the New York *Evening Post*. "This evening for the first time in America, the semi-serious opera of 'Il Don Giovanni,'" reads the advertisement of that date. Then follows the cast. Manuel Garcia played the title rôle; Manuel Garcia, Jr., afterwards inventor of the laryngoscope, who reached the age of 101, dying in London in 1906, was *Leporello;* Mme. Barbieri, *Donna Anna;* Mme. Garcia, *Donna Elvira;* Signorina Maria Garcia (afterwards famous under her married name of Malibran), *Zerlina;* Milon, whom Mr. Krehbiel identifies as a violoncellist later with the Philharmonic Society, *Don Ottavio;* and Carlo Angrisani, *Masetto*, a rôle he had sung at the first London performance of the work.

Da Ponte, the librettist of the work, who had become Professor of Italian at Columbia College, had induced Garcia to put on the opera. At the first performance during the finale of the first act everything went at sixes and sevens, in spite of the efforts of Garcia, in the title rôle, to keep things together. Finally, sword in hand, he stepped to the front of the stage, ordered the performance stopped, and, exhorting the singers not to commit the crime of ruining a masterwork, started the finale over again, which now went all right.

It is related by da Ponte that "my 'Don Giovanni,'" as he called it, made such a success that a friend of his who always fell asleep at operatic performances, not only remained awake during the whole of "Don Giovanni," but told him he couldn't sleep a wink the rest of the night for excitement.

Pauline Viardot-Garcia, sister of Signorina Garcia (afterwards Mme. Malibran), the *Zerlina* of the first New York performance, owned the original autograph score of "Don Giovanni." She bequeathed it to the Paris Conservatoire.

Wolfgang Amadeus Mozart

The opera has engaged the services of famous artists. Faure and Maurel were great *Don Giovannis*, Jean de Reszke sang the rôle, while he was still a baritone; Scotti made his *début* at the Metropolitan Opera House, December 27, 1899, in the rôle, with Nordica as *Donna Anna*, Suzanne Adams, as *Donna Elvira*, Sembrich as *Zerlina*, and Édouard de Reszke as *Leporello*. Renaud appeared as *Don Giovanni* at the Manhattan Opera House. Lablache was accounted the greatest of *Leporellos*. The rôle of *Don Ottavio* has been sung by Rubini and Mario. At the Mozart Festival, Salzburg, 1914, the opera was given with Lilli Lehmann, Farrar, and McCormack in the cast.

A curious aside in the history of the work was an "adaptation," produced by Kalkbrenner in Paris, 1805. How greatly this differed from the original may be judged from the fact that the trio of the masks was sung, not by *Donna Anna, Donna Elvira,* and *Don Ottavio,* but by three policemen!

THE MAGIC FLUTE

DIE ZAUBERFLÖTE

Opera in two acts by Mozart; words by Emanuel Schikaneder and Gieseke. Produced, September 30, 1791, in Vienna, in the Theatre auf der Wieden; Paris, 1801, as "Les Mystères d'Isis"; London, King's Theatre, June 6, 1811 (Italian); Covent Garden, May 27, 1833 (German); Drury Lane, March 10, 1838 (English); New York, Park Theatre, April 17, 1833 (English). The rôle of *Astrofiammante, Queen of the Night*, has been sung here by Carlotta Patti, Ilma di Murska, Gerster, Sembrich, and Hempel.

CHARACTERS

SARASTRO, High Priest of Isis............................*Bass*
TAMINO, an Egyptian Prince...........................*Tenor*
PAPAGENO, a bird-catcher..............................*Baritone*
ASTROFIAMMANTE, Queen of the Night....................*Soprano*
PAMINA, her daughter....................................*Soprano*

The Complete Opera Book

MONOSTATOS, a Moor, chief slave of the Temple...........*Baritone*
PAPAGENA...*Soprano*
Three Ladies-in-Waiting to the Queen; Three Youths of the Temple;
　　　　Priests, Priestesses, Slaves, etc.
Time—Egypt, about the reign of Rameses I.
Place—Near and at the Temple of Isis, Memphis.

The libretto to "The Magic Flute" is considered such a jumble of nonsense that it is as well to endeavour to extract some sense from it.

Emanuel Johann Schikaneder, who wrote it with the aid of a chorister named Gieseke, was a friend of Mozart and a member of the same Masonic Lodge. He also was the manager of a theatrical company and had persuaded Mozart to compose the music to a puppet show for him. He had selected for this show the story of "Lulu" by Liebeskind, which had appeared in a volume of Oriental tales brought out by Wieland under the title of "Dschinnistan." In the original tale a wicked sorcerer has stolen the daughter of the Queen of Night, who is restored by a Prince by means of magic. While Schikaneder was busy on his libretto, a fairy story by Perinet, music by Wenzel Müller, and treating of the same subject, was given at another Viennese theatre. Its great success interfered with Schikaneder's original plan.

At that time, however, freemasonry was a much discussed subject. It had been interdicted by Maria Theresa and armed forces were employed to break up the lodges. As a practical man Schikaneder saw his chance to exploit the interdicted rites on the stage. Out of the wicked sorcerer he made *Sarastro*, the sage priest of Isis. The ordeals of *Tamino* and *Pamina* became copies of the ceremonials of freemasonry. He also laid the scene of the opera in Egypt, where freemasonry believes its rites to have originated. In addition to all this Mozart's beautiful music ennobled the libretto even in its dull and unpoetical

Wolfgang Amadeus Mozart

passages, and lent to the whole a touch of the mysterious and sacred. "The muse of Mozart lightly bears her century of existence," writes a French authority, of this score.

Because of its supposed relation to freemasonry, commentators have identified the vengeful *Queen of the Night* with Maria Theresa, and *Tamino* with the Emperor. *Pamina*, *Papageno*, and *Papagena* are set down as types of the people, and *Monostatos* as the fugleman of monasticism.

Mozart wrote on "The Magic Flute" from March until July and in September, 1791. September 30, two months before his death, the first performance was given.

In the overture to "The Magic Flute" the heavy reiterated chords represent, it has been suggested, the knocking at the door of the lodge room, especially as they are heard again in the temple scene, when the novitiate of *Tamino* is about to begin. The brilliancy of the fugued allegro often has been commented on as well as the resemblance of its theme to that of Clementi's sonata in B-flat.

The story of "The Magic Flute" opens Act I, with *Tamino* endeavouring to escape from a huge snake. He trips in running and falls unconscious. Hearing his cries for help, three black-garbed *Ladies-in-Waiting* of the *Queen of the Night* appear and kill the snake with their spears. Quite unwillingly they leave the handsome youth, who, on recovering consciousness, sees dancing toward him an odd-looking man entirely covered with feathers. It is *Papageno*, a bird-catcher. He tells the astonished *Tamino* that this is the realm of the *Queen of the Night*. Nor, seeing that the snake is dead, does he hesitate to boast that it was he who killed the monster. For this lie he is immediately punished. The three *Ladies-in-Waiting* reappear and place a padlock on his mouth. Then they show *Tamino* the miniature of a maiden, whose magical beauty at once fills his heart with ardent love. Enter the

The Complete Opera Book

Queen of the Night. She tells *Tamino* the portrait is that of her daughter, *Pamina*, who has been taken from her by a wicked sorcerer, *Sarastro*. She has chosen *Tamino* to deliver the maiden and as a reward he will receive her hand in marriage. The *Queen* then disappears and the three *Ladies-in-Waiting* come back. They take the padlock from *Papageno's* mouth, give him a set of chimes and *Tamino* a golden flute. By the aid of these magical instruments they will be able to escape the perils of their journey, on which they will be accompanied by three youths or genii.

Change of scene. A richly furnished apartment in *Sarastro's* palace is disclosed. A brutal Moor, *Monastatos*, is pursuing *Pamina* with unwelcome attentions. The appearance of *Papageno* puts him to flight. The birdcatcher recognizes *Pamina* as the daughter of the *Queen of the Night*, and assures her that she will soon be rescued. In the meantime the *Three Youths* guide *Tamino* to a grove where three temples stand. He is driven away from the doors of two, but at the third there appears a priest who informs him that *Sarastro* is no tyrant, no wicked sorcerer as the *Queen* had warned him, but a man of wisdom and of noble character.

The sound of *Papageno's* voice arouses *Tamino* from the meditations inspired by the words of the priest. He hastens forth and seeks to call his companion by playing on his flute. *Papageno* is not alone. He is trying to escape with *Pamina*, but is prevented by the appearance of *Monostatos* and some slaves, who endeavour to seize them. But *Papageno* sets the Moor and his slaves dancing by playing on his magic chimes.

Trumpet blasts announce the coming of *Sarastro*. *Pamina* falls at the feet of the High Priest and explains that she was trying to escape the unwelcome attentions of the Moor. The latter now drags *Tamino* in, but instead of

Wolfgang Amadeus Mozart

the reward he expects, receives a sound flogging. By the command of *Sarastro*, *Tamino* and *Pamina* are brought into the Temple of Ordeals, where they must prove that they are worthy of the higher happiness.

Act II. In the Palm Grove. *Sarastro* informs the priests of the plans which he has laid. The gods have decided that *Pamina* shall become the wife of the noble youth *Tamino*. *Tamino*, however, must prove, by his own power, that he is worthy of admission to the Temple. Therefore *Sarastro* has taken under his protection *Pamina*, daughter of the *Queen of the Night*, to whom is due all darkness and superstition. But the couple must go through severe ordeals in order to be worthy of entering the Temple of Light, and thus of thwarting the sinister machinations of the *Queen*.

In the succeeding scenes we see these fabulous ordeals, which *Tamino*, with the assistance of his magic flute and his own purity of purpose, finally overcomes in company with *Pamina*. Darkness is banished and the young couple enter into the light of the Temple of the Sun. *Papageno* also fares well, for he receives *Papagena* for wife.

There is much nonsense and even buffoonery in "The Magic Flute"; and, in spite of real nobility in the rôle and music of *Sarastro*, Mr. Krehbiel's comment that the piece should be regarded as somewhat in the same category as a Christmas pantomime is by no means far-fetched. It lends itself to elaborate production, and spectacular performances of it have been given at the Metropolitan Opera House.

Its representation requires for the rôle of *Astrofiammante*, *Queen of the Night,* a soprano of extraordinarily high range and agility of voice, as each of the two great airs of this vengeful lady extend to high F and are so brilliant in style that one associates with them almost anything but the dire outpouring of threats their text is intended to convey.

4

The Complete Opera Book

They were composed because Mozart's sister-in-law, Josepha Weber (Mme. Hofer) was in the cast of the first performance and her voice was such as has been described above. The *Queen* has an air in Act I and another in Act II. A quotation from the second, the so-called "Vengeance aria," will show the range and brilliancy of voice required of a singer in the rôle of *Astrofiammante*.

One is surprised to learn that this *tour de force* of brilliant vocalization is set to words beginning: "Vengeance of hell is boiling in my bosom"; for by no means does it boil with a vengeance.

Papageno in his dress of feathers is an amusing character. His first song, "A fowler bold in me you see," with interludes on his pipes, is jovial; and after his mouth has been padlocked his inarticulate and oft-repeated "Hm!" can always be made provocative of laughter. With *Pamina* he has a charming duet "The manly heart that love desires." The chimes with which he causes *Monostatos* and his slaves to dance, willy-nilly, are delightful and so is his duet with *Papagena*, near the end of the opera. *Tamino*, with the magic flute, charms the wild beasts. They come forth from their lairs and lie at his feet. "Thy magic tones shall speak for me," is his principal air. The concerted number for *Pamina* and trio of female voices (the *Three Youths* or genii) is of exceeding grace. The two *Men in Armour*, who in one of the scenes of the ordeals guard the portal to a subterranean cavern and announce to *Tamino* the awards that await him, do so to the vocal strains of an old German sacred melody with much admired counterpoint in the orchestra.

Next, however, in significance to the music for *Astro-*

Wolfgang Amadeus Mozart

fiammante and, indeed, of far nobler character than the airs for the *Queen of the Night*, are the invocation of Isis by *Sarastro*, "O, Isis and Osiris," with its interluding chant of the priests, and his air, "Within this hallowed dwelling." Not only the solemnity of the vocal score but the beauty of the orchestral accompaniment, so rich, yet so restrained, justly cause these two numbers to rank with Mozart's finest achievements.

"Die Zauberflöte" (The Magic Flute) was its composer's swan-song in opera and perhaps his greatest popular success. Yet he is said to have made little or nothing out of it, having reserved as his compensation the right to dispose of copies of the score to other theatres. Copies, however, were procured surreptitiously; his last illness set in; and, poor business man that he was, others reaped the rewards of his genius.

In 1801, ten years after Mozart's death, there was produced in Paris an extraordinary version of "The Magic Flute," entitled "Les Mystères d'Isis" (The Mysteries of Isis). Underlying this was a considerable portion of "The Magic Flute" score, but also introduced in it were fragments from other works of the composer ("Don Giovanni," "Figaro," "Clemenza di Tito") and even bits from Haydn symphonies. Yet this hodge-podge not only had great success—owing to the magic of Mozart's music—it actually was revived more than a quarter of a century later, and the real "Zauberflöte" was not given in Paris until 1829.

Besides the operas discussed, Mozart produced (1781) "Idomoneo" and (1791) "La Clemenza di Tito." In 1768, when he was twelve years old, a one-act "Singspiel" or musical comedy, "Bastien and Bastienne," based on a French vaudeville by Mme. Favart, was privately played in Vienna. With text rearranged by Max Kalbeck, the graceful little piece has been revived with success. The

The Complete Opera Book

story is of the simplest. Two lovers, *Bastien* (tenor) and *Bastienne* (soprano), have quarrelled. Without the slightest complication in the plot, they are brought together by the third character, an old shepherd named *Colas* (bass). "Der Schauspiel-director" (The Impresario), another little comedy opera, produced 1786, introduces that clever rogue, Schikaneder, at whose entreaty "The Magic Flute" was composed. The other characters include Mozart himself, and Mme. Hofer, his sister-in-law, who was the *Queen of the Night* in the original cast of "The Magic Flute." The story deals with the troubles of an impresario due to the jealousy of prima donnas. "Before they are engaged, opera singers are very engaging, except when they are engaged in singing." This line is from H. E. Krehbiel's translation of the libretto, produced, with "Bastien and Bastienne" (translated by Alice Matullah, as a "lyric pastoral"), at the Empire Theatre, New York, October 26, 1916. These charming productions were made by the Society of American Singers with a company including David Bispham (Schikaneder and Colas), Albert Reiss (Mozart and Bastien), Mabel Garrison, and Lucy Gates; the direction that of Mr. Reiss.

There remain to be mentioned two other operatic comedies by Mozart: "The Elopement from the Serail" (Belmonte und Constance), 1782, in three acts; and "Così fan Tutte" (They All Do It), 1790, in two. The music of "Così fan Tutte" is so sparkling that various attempts have been made to relieve it of the handicap imposed by the banality of the original libretto by da Ponte. Herman Levi's version has proven the most successful of the various rearrangements. The characters are two Andalusian sisters, *Fiordiligi* (soprano), *Dorabella* (soprano); two officers, their fiancés, *Ferrando* (tenor), and *Guglielmo* (baritone); *Alfonso* (bass); and *Despina* (soprano), maid to the two sisters.

Wolfgang Amadeus Mozart

Alfonso lays a wager with the officers that, like all women, their fiancées will prove unfaithful, if opportunity were offered. The men pretend their regiment has been ordered to Havana, then return in disguise and lay siege to the young ladies. In various ways, including a threat of suicide, the women's sympathies are played upon. In the original they are moved to pledge their hearts and hands to the supposed new-comers. A reconciliation follows their simple pronouncement that "they all do it."

In the revised version, they become cognizant of the intrigue, play their parts in it knowingly, at the right moment disclose their knowledge, shame their lovers, and forgive them. An actual wager laid in Vienna is said to have furnished the basis for da Ponte's libretto.

www.ingramcontent.com/pod-product-compliance
Lightning Source LLC
Chambersburg PA
CBHW022123090426
42743CB00008B/982